Collected Poems from The Poetry Society of Virginia

Liste

And who was left, a

Breathe

exit

ry or not

ead careful

And what of the

insanity

Embodied in the spirit

d fancy

shall Lenore

mindlessness

mind

the room, silent

graveyard

listen

heartbeat, alas

Behind my

Poetry

Virginia

2021

First Edition 2022

Published by High Tide Publications, Inc.
Deltaville, Virginia
www.HighTidePublications.com

Graphic Arts: Firebelliedfrog.com
Printed in the United States of America.

ISBN: 978-1-945990-63-2

Congratulations to all the winners of the 2021 PSV Annual Poetry Contest! We are thrilled to present our yearly book of winners, including upper school students.

So, why publish a book of winning entries? Publishing not only validates poets, it gives others a sense of what wins. Having said that, we rarely use the same judges for the same categories. The standard is simple: whether the poem is strong, not whether it is to the judge's taste.

The book is also entertaining, elucidating and useful as a work of its own.

What sort of work shines? How to choose a theme? The Poe category is wide open. Others, such as the Bess Gresham Memorial, have a theme.

Notes for future contests: if your poem did not place in any if the categories, you may resubmit it in a different category the following year. We try our best to mix-and-match the judges. We are asking winners of any single contest to skip a year before submitting to that specific category again, to give others a chance to shine.

"In "Virtual, in this Lonely Space," the 2021 1st place winner, Erin Newton Wells writes,

> A flowering branch touches jeweled water.
> Tell me how it looks, you prompt,
> and say
> you never see it as I do until I say it,
> the branch painted on silk and its wet
> colors run. We carry on for weeks, months,
> too long. ...
> we carry on with what we can, patching
> together the world we used to know."

In a similar vein of nature, color and connectedness, high-schooler Lacy Powell writes,

> "Her skin nurtures and is nurtured—of greens, blues, and yellows.
> And every life has roots that run deep.
> Every event leads back to her..."

Both poets use specifics, both touch on the universal. Their rhythms and line breaks differ. Yet both deliver a profound message of their own in just a few lines. Good poetry does that--creates and carries a message that crosses boundaries in a few, well-placed words.

I hope that this volume will delight, awaken, and inspire you.

Terry Cox-Joseph, President, 2021
Poetry Society of Virginia

Categories and Winners

The Poetry Society of Virginia

Advancing the cause of Virginia's Poetry since 1923.

First Place

Donna Isaac
Letting Go

When wind in pied trees sighs
they have not long
their hold on gold.

A nun said "Lost time is never found."

Autumn is here. I must escape to the mountains.
I am masked and gloved and flying.

I have a nephew in prison,
let's call him Lee. His mother
will be 80 the day he's out.

Lee plays the drums like Lars Ulrich
but with covid he lost music room
privileges. He eats baloney sandwiches in his cell.

The staff refused a hardback book
about Metallica I sent him.
Soft covers only.

They sent back a letter
with an address sticker
also several birthday cards.

Lee's had an infected toe-nail
over three months.

Once I couldn't enter the prison
because of my open-back shoes.
When there's fog, prisoners are locked down.

Two rivers flow nearby.
An abattoir of shrikes, a bouquet of warblers,
shrouds over a southern battlefield.

A little boy collects rust and reddish leaves.
He pastes them in a book where the glue
will harden, the leaves, crack.

I sip red wine ringed by the Big House range.

A blue moon is rising soon.

Second Place

M. Lee Alexander
Domestic Drama on Lake Iroquois
(Why Great-Aunt Isobel's Cottage Is For Sale)

Act I: Anticipation

You swore the cabin wouldn't smell this year:
we'd go in early and air out the den
and let the lake breeze in, and haul the beer
kegs out from when your nephew and his friends
usurped the cottage for their birthday bash.
You'd been there since and said it was a wreck
(and frankly was an offense to the nose)
but we could scrub the halls and swab the deck!
So we stuffed our duffel bags with comfy clothes,
and hit the ATM for extra cash.
We bought a crate of cheap but cheerful wine,
bid farewell to the house and we were gone
hightailing out on Highway 89 . . .
determined we would make it there by dawn.

Act II: Arrival

We didn't stop and made it there by dawn,
and let our Labrador go bounding out
onto the pier and leap about the lawn
while we set out to make the hut a home.
We divvied up the tasks to make it fair;
I started in the bedroom, changing sheets
but in the pillowcase a necklace flashed
that wasn't mine, with twisted strands of hair
dyed red that didn't match my grey, and then
the dizzying image of your office mate
came spinning like a whirlwind through my mind,
because this was a situation that

4

you'd also said would not occur again—
I've got to stop believing Harvard men.

Act III: Alma Mater

I've got to stop believing Harvard men,
those lettered in that legendary place.
So many years have passed since first we met
as freshmen starting out our paper chase.
It seems so strange to think what we were then,
for those seemed halcyon days that would not end
of Frisbees flying in the quad and boom-
box blaring from the windowsills of dorm
rooms full of secrets; dances and debates
past midnight every night, and posters on the wall:
but Harvard's motto "Veritas" did not extend
to your faint heart had I but known it then.
A gentleman and scholar, I supposed:
your books were open, but your heart was closed.

Act IV: Arbitration / Aggravation / Acceptance

Your books were open but your heart was closed.
And now you feed on paperbacks and light
Sudoku when you have the time, but claim
your workload keeps you later every night.
So though I see you bent hard in the clench
of cleaning the Aegean Stables, broom
in hand, pine-sol attacking every room,
and muscles flexing as you chop the wood,
and sunshine glinting off the waters cool—
I think that I have finally understood
you are a lifelong liar as the stench
of infidelity that fills my nose
annuls our cleaning object all sublime:
as I'd been such a fatuous five-star fool
to flout the redhead hussy in this rhyme./ Time dime climb crime grime
fulltime.

Act V: Alternate View

(OK so I'm the redhead in this tale:
The missy telling it is not so chaste
as she might have us think. Let facts prevail:
for she's a rival easily replaced.
She isn't any dream wife, that's for sure:
she's just a dreadful cook, and getting fat.
The truth is that her thoughts were far from pure—
she didn't always see his needs were met,
and sometimes too her eye would slyly stray
to other men in their gymkhana set.
Perhaps she didn't act upon those thoughts
but the desire was there, say what she may.
They say that love in faith and trust abides—
The truth is there were full faults on both sides.)

Act VI: Animal Attraction / Animation / Acceptance

It's not true that the faults were on both sides,
as you were always champing at the bit.
From early on I had to watch my back
and hope that you would finally tire of your
stenographers and stable girls galore.
You promised the parade was over, and
I prayed we'd finally reached the end of it.
I should have known the day we got the cat
who purred and pawed his way into our lives
that you were going to be a guy like that
who quickly tires of newfound loves and tries
to think of reasons to renege; you claimed
your allergies were fierce and going strong—
but I felt you were faking all along.

Act VII: Arrivederci

I felt that you were faking all along
but lulled myself into believing lies,
to dance along to lyrics of a song
that shifts until its own theme nullifies.

So as my lover stretches and unpacks,
and smiles at me across the unmade bed
and feasts on blackberries fresh-picked from the vine
and pancakes drowned in Maple syrup tapped
from local trees that now in glorious hues
burst forth with phony promises of joy
and gladness burning in the autumn sky,
I contemplate a new use for that axe . . .
because my untrue darling and my dear—
you *swore* the cabin wouldn't smell this year!

First Place

Julia Travers
More

I'm not a sofa sheeted by a host,
saved for some later day -- my life is more --
I'm no invention turned to hoarded ghost.
I'm not a bat unswung, a dress unworn.

No ivory tablecloth -- I won't just fold
and softly start to mold in quiet drawers,
forgotten, quartered neatly, growing old.
No family heirloom here -- my life is more;

not a diploma framed in dusty glass
or album of another year and face.
I will not moor myself to years now past,
and leave today unplayed, unspent, a waste.

I'll be a flag that flies the air in tatters;
a glass which, dropped from merry fingers, shatters.

Second Place

Edward Wright Haile
Marry Me

"Marry me and marry agony
and warts, and one who lives in a bad novel
of dreary days and pointless attitudes,
the moreso since to me they are so precious.
You'll not disturb them with impunity.
Each week this home turns back into a hovel
of comfortable arrangements, if it suits
my Monday's woman to make it less infectious.
From the clear black of love's astronomy,
I'd say, expect most perfect nights to travel
back to our stale interiors where we've screwed
our bright particulars," so he confesses,
and all his ladies have stated their desires
to break off there and marry better liars.

First Place

Erin Newton Wells
Virtual, In This Lonely Space

What I want to tell you when you send
that first frame is how it looks blue-green.

Is it really, or a miracle of light. If there,
would I see it aquamarine, your pond

a pond in the gardens of Monet, daydream,
idyll. You send another, the same cool

green and dappled blue, to prove its truth,
and I print it for my solitary house

where I shelter in place. Imagine us, hats
with large pale brims. We dabble our toes.

A flowering branch touches jeweled water.
The tiny island holds a nest, the goose

who returns every year and builds a tower
of sticks. You send several of this.

Tell me how it looks, you prompt, and say
you never see it as I do until I say it,

the branch painted on silk and its wet
colors run. We carry on for weeks, months,

too long. It will be a year or more, friend,
until I see you. Your pictures, my words,

we carry on with what we can, patching
together the world we used to know.

Second Place

Sarah Kohrs
By a Kenyan Campfire

Like a light-soaked shell
with its
inverse braille tatted in
cream & peach
& amethyst,

sky cradles sun after
its hike over
ridges buoyed by
blue, hatchmarked in
shadow.

Knotted stitches fasten night   overhead
while cricket song subdues the   wildness. Earlier,

the local haberdasher sold
me
Maasai plaid stacked on
shelves that filled every
wall—

windowless, with only
one door
in or out. I wrap that
cloth around my body
like a

buffalo hide and
watch as flame
licks the air and
smoke settles in the
bias.

It first started with
the touch of
a torch brought from
the kitchen fire,
where

ugali gummed up like water-in-fat   balls
and *sukuma wiki* & *mbuzi mchuzi*   simmered

in deep kettles. In that moment, as   precious
as Morpho wings or the shrill of a   conch pressed

to lips or sweet sap pulled
from a
honeysuckle bell, our
faces glow with the same
ethereal

milkiness that transcends   a moment.
Our stories mingle, even if   the words

our Adams gave us differ. We're   settled
in the shell's convexity as if in a   cupped palm.

Held there, weaving
grass that
shimmers like river
chalk, whose dust coats
even us.

First Place

Stuart Gunter
Clearing Wood

Five beers in, I'm clearing wood, loading it
behind our red barn, or what we call the barn,
this old shed, leaning from time's dark progress.

A waxing moon, night clear as glass. Cold.
In the distance: the unmistakable bark
of a goose winging down the Rockfish River.

I stack these logs my wife and I split. The saw
blazed through the old fallen oak, and we hauled
and threw and loaded and split some more.

Now I'm half-drunk cleaning up behind my run-down
old shed on this cold, crisp night, wondering about a goose.

Second Place

Donna Isaac
Picking Asparagus

In early spring tiny blades of green
cut through mudwash and mulch,
breaking through to form first hyacinths,
daffodils, and tulips. On the north
side of the mountain, three leaves
of ramps, along the roadside
first thin spears of asparagus.
My sister and I pull the car over
to pick the spindles,
taking them home to blanch or roast
with oil, butter, lemon zest,
overeating since they were *gratis,*
bountiful, spinning them into grassy soup
dotted with sorrel or dill, a dollop
of sour cream, reliving consumption,
urine, sulfurous and rank,
but moods elevated, bones
stronger, energy, boosted enough
to re-dig in mud, to forage for what is wild.

First Place

William Prindle
University Village: Etudes

i.
The pink weight of dawn
pushes down the blue
      edge of night
      making the lights
of the retirement home
on the ridge over the river
      glitter copper.

Anne is back in Johnstown,
January 1945, curled up
with the radio voice of Roosevelt,
      avuncular honey flowing
      from the big brown
Philco in the empty living room.
Still no word from Derek
      with the Screaming Eagles
      in the Ardennes Forest.

In her state of mind the staff agree
      not to try
to explain to her that the Nazis
      are back.
The unfiltered sun through
the floor-length windows
is fierce enough and merciful
      enough to sear
      her memory shut.

ii.
On the ridge over the river
the retirement home windows
     glow copper
     again in the dawn
as the breastplate of Hector
must have shone while he waited
     for Achilles.

Hank drifts in and out of the same
dream of the slender Japanese boy,
     more like a girl,
     really, the one
he bayonetted behind the beach
     on Saipan
     after Ernie
took it in the belly from the kid's
     machine gun.

His daughter is bringing the grandkids
     for lunch. Zack
in fifth grade is obsessed with WWII
     weaponry of all kinds,
wants to know if the machine gun
     was Type 11
     or Type 21.

iii.
Though the windows of my father's
New Jersey Sunrise room never glowed
     copper at dawn,
or if they did he would not have seen
     such glory
from his wheelchair inside, perhaps

he dreamt of his summer honeymoon
     of 1940,
sailing the Bay on the True Love
     with my mother,
or was it of that girl he knew in school?

Or the sleepy San Juan Sunday
when the chief petty officer ran up
          waving a telegram
saying Pearl Harbor had been bombed,
          he wondering
'where the hell Is Pearl Harbor?'

Or the boredom of tug escort duty
circling the old tub over and over,
          as perhaps he protected
          us, steadily
and at a distance, the ensign furling
itself around the mast, he reversing course
          to unfurl the flag
          one more time?

Second Place

Jerri Hardesty
The Navajo Code Talkers

We are loyal warriors.
We have used the magic
Of our sacred tongue
To help defend
This nation
We are now a part of.
We have used the very same
Language
That brought us
Punishment
When it spilled from our lips
In the Catholic schools.
To protect
The right to choose
How to worship.
We are freedom of speech.
See the great spirit
Laughing
At the irony.
The wheel of life
Has come full circle.
See the smoke signals
Of our ancestors.
Thunderbirds rising
In the blasts
Of artillery canons.

First Place

Amyrah Gray Young
Redwing, 1888

Alone at night, four candles lit, I spin.
No one must know my source of silk, where all
my neighbors' fears and prayers combine. It's in
this place with wide-framed mirrors on each wall
I generate the dreams this tight town needs.
They're red where crimson's called for, blue where sky
wants rising wings, smooth black for broken seeds
that yield a lifetime's *how* and *why*.
What do I know? My fingers sing the wheel
hearts turn for me in words they dare not say.
Small room, high window, all the breaths I feel:
they come together at the close of day.
I'm shadow. Silver. And when I am dead
another will embrace these spools for thread.

Second Place

JM Jordan

Chinatown Sonnet
Sonnet At The Red Victoria

O neon can-can city, grinning
coquette, O block-bright hilltops!
The fanfare never slacks or stops.
We burn the tonic daylight spinning

from place to muralled place, pin-balling
from street to track to clattering cab,
all bebop glitz and techie shab.
We push it all to the point of falling.

A room at last. White curtains blow
across the bed in the pale lamp light.
We fall in utter done-ness, utter

grace, while the sirens down below
wail in the damn disastrous night
and the street-punks fight in the gutter.

First Place

Erin Newton Wells
Oracle Of Bronzeville Meets Herself

Gwendolyn Brooks at Kenwood Park, Chicago

Floating through, I find it at Forty-Fifth and Greenwood,
a nice breeze from shore, a hint of back porch
behind me. Here I am, finger to my head
about to tell you what I think.
Sit down on a boulder. I invite you,
just half of me on a block, but enough for the job.
They call me an oracle
so I guess I speak from the air.
One thing they got right and made it bronze.

This is where I come back or never left,
given anywhere to choose, a drive farther north
to look at golden gardens
and people who live long enough to have white hair.
But this is where I reappear. Bronzeville.
We die young here. Except
sometimes it takes a little longer.

They pull a quilt off my head and make a big fuss
for my birthday, this bronze self.
I would be a hundred and one. Thank God to see
the hair natural for eternity.

The best part is children. Bring them, as many as you can.
I look them in the eye and tell them
they shine,
can do anything, have the world. Start here, right here
in Bronzeville.
I tell them I love them, love them all,
even the ones we lost. They rise from the ground.

21

Second Place

Donna Isaac
Taco King

Maria taps me on the head with an empty box,
"For luck," she says and goes on stuffing
tacos with ground beef, lettuce, cheese,
and a perfect soupcon of diced tomato.
She plays the Gypsy Kings on a cassette player,
hums, and sways, turning to heat refried beans
in the microwave, stirring the mush after the ding.
There's a line down the block, customers staring
 at the Texas-born *senoras* building burritos and nachos grande,
filling up bottles of fresh salsa loved for its afterburn.
They speak Spanish amongst themselves, and we gringos
try a few words like *queso, pollo,* and *frijoles.*
Their many children come around and hang out
in the back supply tent, sampling tostadas drizzled
with hot liquid cheese and jumbo Mountain Dews.
"I just love this place," a woman wearing pig ears
exclaims. "It's my first stop at the Fair!"
Others want the fresh salsa recipe which the ladies tell them
is easy with a super duper blender, tomato filets,
white onions, and jalapenos. That's all it is after all.
Oh, and a little salt. At the end of the day, fireworks bursting,
a trickle of drunks orders what's left of the burritos.
Maria pulls out the last tissue to wrap the last taco,
knocks me on the head with the box and says,
"Por suerte." A street cleaner whirrs brushes on the pavement.
A mélange of chicken bits, plastic trays, corn chips,
and lettuce strips go 'round and 'round. All the hard-working
women walk to their cars. Luck has nothing to do with it.

First Place

Ellaraine Lockie
Pretense

As a child I pretended their intolerance was ignorance
Racism too ugly a brand to mar
my perception of perfect Montana farm people
when bigotry crept like weeds into crops of wheat
Passed down from eighth-grade-educated parents
with God-fearing goodness
But hailing hypocrisy when
Harlem Globetrotters needed housing
And were banished to the next bucolic county
Where toddlers were told to wash
because Indians may have held that half dollar
And where malice still wars with mixed marriages
I pretended their intolerance was inexperience
The only exposure inherited
from history's deep South
Reinforced by racial slurs
and ethnic insults hoodwinked as humor
I pretended until the whitewash
ran red from sins of ancestors
From discrimination that pre-dates the Civil War
When founding fathers fenced Native Americans
Roping them off in reservation corrals
With federal guilt funding that couldn't convert
to American middle class
Or compensate for a lost way of life
Altered over time into alcoholism
poverty and apathy
A hundred years of segregation
preceding their one saloon in town
An offering locals consider liberal
And anyone who thinks it's not enough

Second Place tie

Tom Jenkins
Where Should I Walk?

When all of nature's beauty,
With countless lighted dancers dancing
Across her every wonders rim,
Are caught reflections of every within.

When love turns thoughts into fountains,
And skies into blue beyonds.
When we have love waiting
In the blue beyonds in us.

When every song never written
Till it's heard in the air.
When there is always knowing
And glimpses of joy and trust everywhere.

When each soul that walks beside,
Carries universes of ours and more
With them in volumes unseen.
When the all in every way is in every reach.
When each soul knows, touches and speaks.

Second Place tie

Pamela Brothers Denyes
Explode like Lightning Striking

Because we have so few trees now
But so many cell phones,
I saw a man lynched, murdered
Under the knee of another man,
Just another angry man.

The few trees and many mothers
Cry out in remembrance, in
Recognition of Cain slaying
Abel all over again. How many
Can the crying mothers and the

All-seeing trees take inside
Of their bodies before they
Explode like lightning striking,
From anguish, pain of generations
Of saplings, cut down in their prime?
Who can blame them?

First Place

Sharon Ackerman
A Thing Nearly Perfect

An orb weaver's sphere
leaves no thread to dangle,
no visible beginning or end, lace
cross-hatched in circles
our fingers can't make or draw,
graced by a slant of sun.
Light-catcher hung leaf to leaf
suspended round
as a communion plate, whose offering
bids us stop and know
a labor made of not just one motion,
but many shining. So that
we wish to see it in the moon's
light as well, silver and scalloped,
life's longing backlit in pearls
so that reflection halts
the breath and though
a calling away will come
and none of us
can stay long in that hush,
to stand still a moment and say *goddamn*
becomes prayer enough.

Second Place

Andy Fogle
Looking At The Floor At Saratoga Friends Meeting House

Hands clasped, elbows on knees,
face three feet from centuries-
old floor, happy for
a smaller world, I watch
a spider play the woodgrains.
Next to bench-leg, a dead
cellar spider covered in web

decays into what it's made.
A strand wavers in breeze.
An Asian Lady Beetle
wobbles along plank grains.
When it finds the seam between two,
its path straightens, and it follows
that seam out of my sight.

Crows' caws riffle from beyond
as a dome of cricketsound
cakebells this house, descends
like a net, their glitter of clicks
a sheen beneath the other sounds:
horse whinny, jay screech, a low whine
I can't yet recognize.

First Place

Sharon Ackerman
Vernal Equinox

Despite this burgeoning
the periphery holds;
how nicely the world obliges
new petals, the green shove
insisting on itself
first, above all. Beautiful.

Soon cherry blossoms will mock
the dead, the season fight
for its young, as from the beginning
of time, the weakest pup
edged off the breast
      ---I want my milk! Such bald

fierceness locks into place
the tenderest shoot,
drills through hardened clay
and sidewalk, every crack
unfurls a fresh minted flower's
capacity for surprise.

I thought I was done with love---
but no, it all comes back doesn't it?
Just as Spring bends on one knee
offering emeralds.

Second Place

Coral Kendall
I Want You To Come Back But Only If You're Full

If you could hold me right now
You'd sense the volcanic aftershock of an abandoned city
That pulse beneath my hands squeezes yours
like it's the only piano its ever played properly
Meaning my pulse doesn't know
What melody sounds like or how it starts,
Just whatever you hold inside once it's over, but not breath

Loving conditionally is like inviting gravity to the moon,
Expect a jump that asks, "High enough yet, Hun?"
Like kissing goodbye couldn't mean a tongue wrestle
For the prize of finding a home to let
Past-Life kick his feet up on the desk every night
With someone lying in their bed waiting
And just waiting
For him to turn the light out instead

To me, your absence makes for
An empty room that used to be my favorite,
It was plopped in the center of a house big enough
To fill your lungs with and then throw a lump in it,
Enough oxygen to feed the ocean
When no one asked you to, ever

If someone had asked me before
To fly with them instead of for them,
I would've spent the rest of my life
Floating along streets I'd never remember the names of
Instead, I'd change my name to a child's I'll never raise,
Let go of the heartbeat that never
Asked my opinion in the first place
Become a traveler that could never decide

Between going and staying
So instead asked someone to do both
While I pretend to never hear the question

First Place

Rebecca Leet
Weathering

Not even hunger
brings them to a feeder
swinging wildly   bobbing
like a buoy storm-tossed
on waves of the Chesapeake.

No mourning dove
no purple finch
no chickadee.

They wait someplace safe
for the gale to calm.

The feeder dangles from a white pine
whose thinner branches
bounce twist   flip
acquiescing

until winds are spent
routine returns.

At the window,
cloistered alone
against rampant pandemic,
I take notes   on weathering
what I cannot control.

Second Place

Deborah Baxter
In a Dogwood Tree

The nest is empty now; the mother bird saw me
one too many times as I leaned over the porch railing.
I glimpsed her as she sat on her masterpiece, brown
like her, as brown as last year's grasses and woven
into a soft home for the robin's blue eggs she warmed.

Later, her babies hatched, naked as humans, helpless,
hungry for the world and for flight. Leaving almost as
soon as they arrived, they grasped the dogwood's
branches tightly with clawed feet, fluttered their wings,
soaring into the blue world without faltering or fear.

First Place

Robert Keeler
**Ode to the Young Construction Worker Who Once Placed a
Loaded Nail Gun against His Forehead and Pulled the Trigger**

I did not raise, much less ever love, orchids.
Feathers in the mind; the deserts inside merciless and extensive.
So many downed trees, and out ahead only black salt.
It was Sunday, not a work day, the job site was quiet, I went in alone.
I remember waters all moving, and I with them.
I strike that day; once in a while, though, I get a glimpse.
I learned early that you killed your gods, then ate them.
Such was my indictment.

Wind at my back, hosannas, everything steadily rising up.
My horoscope was three luminous planets in alignment; blessedness and
unction abound.
My sixty-five years were full, my course like a clear and meandering
stream.
  That sky-dive, the main parachute cords tangling at 3300 feet, my
  reserve chute opening.
  I met Lucy at the bottom of a flooded cave. I was out of air; she gave me
  mouth-to-
  mouth, kept on doing it for 34 years. What a champ, came with three
exquisite
  children, everyone laughs a lot.
  After the twins went west to college, she and I commenced adventure
  after adventure.
Now, given any chance, I dance, I pet dogs, twice.

Years ago, I mentioned these exploits to the kids. *Oh, so charmed*, they
laughed.

Second Place

Katherine Gotthardt
Aftermath

3:37 a.m.
I listen for helicopters,
for some staccato pop,
if not, then something banal
I can count to get back to sleep,
perhaps the seconds between
what the clock says,
what the newsman says,
what my mother would say: "Pray."

3:39 a.m.
Horrible as it sounds,
I'm thankful she did not live
to see all that died this day.
Her anxiety would have multiplied,
packed itself tightly against her chest,
pressed the crucifix closer to her skin.
Would she have added more icons
to that thin silver chain?
I try to count my blessings.

3:42 a.m.
I find myself listening for shouting,
some unusual sound, other
than profound replays of chaos,
democracy gone wrong:
the steel barricade widening,
well-oiled gunmen sliding through police,
the breach of the Capitol walls,
climbing the sides of law and order.
I count up slowly, inhale, cry,
start to ask my mother why.

3:44 a.m.
I divide the seconds,
breaking down statements of what we know:
hot mob, conspiracy spread like incense,
tatted man in horns, no shirt, fur pelt,
Confederate flag claiming the mosaic floor.
Not your average person inciting insurrection.
"A nutty," she'd have called him.
Certainly not someone
counting on sleeping that night.

3:49 a.m.
I ask myself if anxiety is inherited,
if a weighted blanket would help.
Not that it matters when
a whole praying world leans in,
heads tilted, listening as I am,
for the sound of everything ending.
Some are counting on it.

3:52 a.m.
I decide it's time I get up,
calculate how to cope,
ask my mother to find the solution,
don my best jewelry and wristwatch.
Let's set an alarm, shall we?
Do something a little different,
this time, count down until dawn.
Keep eyes out the living room window,
watch sunrise stretch its arms.
Watch for horizon again.

First Place

Erin Wells
An Invitation To The Masked Corona Ball

> Your presence is greatly desired
> but only if aptly attired,
> your choice of costume
> with plenty of room
> to give you the distance required.
>
> A space of six feet is enough
> for farthingale, rapier, or ruff,
> and masks, to be sure,
> will be de rigueur
> for all, even those in the buff.

Second Place

Sharon Dorsey
The Great Toilet Paper Caper

There once was a land held at bay
by illness that had come to stay.
We hid in our home,
too fearful to roam,
to wait for a healthy new day.

The virus of darkness did smile,
ran up and down grocery aisle.
What a great caper!
Stole toilet paper,
then hid it away in a pile.

We all wondered why it was gone.
Were we being used as a pawn?
Did powers that be
just trick you and me
into orders from Amazon?

First Place

Erin Wells
Day Of Wind

I think of you, the sea close by, its drum
the last you hear. They told me thread, a spool

of thread. You asked for it, though heaven knows
the use you had just then, the strand in twists

of ecru raveling out across the room.
A silver needle, you would want this too,

though no one said you did, and no one guessed
the dress you meant to make again, its scoop

and flow, the way the fabric swirled when you
were younger than the earth. I think of how

you slipped away, and none of us were there
to hear your words and give you what you asked,

a flounce of it to gather at your waist
and trail the scarves behind you as you reach

the sea, a wind as fresh as silk. I think
of how your fingers smooth it into place,

the gauze of nets in sympathy below
luffed out to feel you pass. Then prominence

of headland, then the last of it, the sea
gone still and white as dream when it dissolves.

Pentecost
Andrew Wyeth
July 12, 1917- January 16, 2009

Second Place

Katharyn Howd Machan
Garien Swift: Redwing, 1888

Skull with Crows
Wall Art
Martin Wagner

I reach for them, the birds, when I feel wrong.
Deep black, widespread, their sharp beaks full of dark
cacophony my terror hears as song:
they are my comfort, alien and stark.

You won't believe the story of my birth.
I won't disclose it. Better just to see
the world the way I view it: startled earth
that shapes the breath and blood and bones of me.

You're quiet now. You realize you should turn
away, pretend you never heard my name?
You haven't even smelled the feathers burn
as I feed clipped wings to my oven's flame.

You think you can dismiss me. Don't you know
I am the tremble of the Devil's crow?

First Place

JM Jordan
Night Is A Dark Unguarded Grove

O Night is a dark unguarded grove
where the gods' luminescent fruit
hangs heavy and ripe to the hand
of the quick, the sly and the willing.

And when you hear that call, my child, that chorus
of wailing siren pulse and distant circus whisper,
then fling your window open, let
the dark wind fill your curtains like sails.

Recite the prayers on your walls,
swear fealty to your family
then swing out, child, out into the darkness
and ride that clattering drain pipe to the ground.

Only be home by morning-time,
before your mother stirs the covers.
Be home to touch her sleeping shoulder
and whisper to her that her dreams for you are true.

Second Place

Erin Wells
The Summer Of Secret Stones

We stayed home, thought of each other. It was the
time
we had to be alone, no one together. We tried

to think of what to do, looked out the window, hoped
to see another looking back.

Sometimes we went out by ourselves to walk the
paths
nearby. The world was silent

except for the wren, cricket and cicada, the wind
that spoke through hickory leaves.

I stepped into the small wood, and this is where I saw
it,
lilac and smooth at my feet,

picked it up, could barely read the tiny words in
pink—
Take me and hide me somewhere else.

On the other side of the wood I left it near a tree.
The next day it was gone, another on a leaf,

three white clouds on blue. Stone by stone, summer
went by. We found them everywhere, began

to paint and leave them. One said, *What music makes
you smile?* Another, *Love is a forest of birds.*

We could feel the hands of others paint and choose,
could think how near.

First Place

Erin Wells
She Whispers How It Ends

This, to me in a dream, her faint migration
across my sleep, what she never tells me as a child,

keeps it in a box of letters, browned paper, garland
of satin rosettes faded colorless.

This, trailed across me as night wind in her voice:
We tie cloth around our faces. Some days

we do not go out—a finger before her mouth.
Shhh. Tell no one about the bodies,

about the beaches. What I heard as a child, the tale
of the milliner's shop,

the upper room, and sea rising at the window.
A new century with two blank aughts.

She, young enough to imagine bodies do not die.
The part about the hats,

her nimble needle, feathers, veils, rosettes.
She teaches me the rhyme. *September/Remember.*

The Gulf a bowl, a strip of sand called Galveston,
storm howling toward it. She,

young enough not to hear or know. The air
smells of tin that day, her long skirt wet with rain.

Someone rows by in a boat and hands her a loaf
through the window. Bread,

a pitcher of water, her nimble fingers, night and sea
outside. And after,

matchsticks piled in dark mountains, the voices
beneath. Tell no one of the orphans

each tied to a line to save them, hands of the sisters
of charity making each knot, a rosary

of children who drown. Of thousands buried at sea
thousands wash back,

thousands on the beach to set on fire. *Hush.*
We tie cloth around our faces. Some days we do not

go out. A bit of silk to keep busy. Hold the center
at the eye. Crimp outward, a swirl.

A blue rosette, a lavender. She pins them in my hair.
Wind, then silence. Pass through the eye.

A heavy scent, sand darkened with char, air heavy
with more than this.

Second Place

Katharyn Howd Machan
When They Left the Cottage Behind

They had always mined the earth
outside the forest where trees grew thin
on mountainside after mountainside,
shadows and lamps defining their days
before and after the shining girl
they gave away to a prince.
Red caps, thick warm beards, hands

steady on shovels and picks
as they knew seasons at dawn and dusk,
sometimes at night if one awoke
to a mating owl, crickets in chorus,
chestnuts dropping, snow pattering glass.
Decades of breath among the seven,
simple meals, shared trips to town

to sell the magic of the ore
that glittered or gleamed in buyers' eyes,
taking the shape world needed most.
So of course when Death tapped one
they all felt it in their bones
and walked together one final time
to the cave they'd hollowed far away

from the reach of their fairy tale. There—
if you're lucky or chosen or blessed—
you may one day wander and hear
echoes of iron on veins of dream
and find—just one—at your weary feet
a stone that glows with Love's real name
you may pick up and hold and keep.

First Place

Claudia Gary
Catheter Ablation

Two hours on the table
his body reclines
arranged as a path

      for cautery's
      snake to enter his
      heart.

Clean current
stamps invisible
scars
to settle his pulse.

      No longer two
      steps ahead and one
      back,

blood coursing
forward oxygen-laden
quickens his brain.

      The serpent
      withdrawn, he gathers
      his wisdom. The serpent withdrawn, he gathers his wisdom.

Second Place

Joan Ellen Casey
New And Repurposed Words

At one time there was only poetic license
to embellish the real world.
Now we have virtual, mixed, and augmented realities,
and those who deal in alt facts.
Just choose a headset, twitter feed, or channel
for the world you want to live in.

At one time we feared loss of memory
now we have too much
with RAM, made of memory chips
formed into a motherboard module,
secretly caching data of all
we forgot or never knew.

Sometimes a virus comes from a bug,
now we can also get one from a group of colluding bots
which crawl websites searching
for foul language among chat room participants.
Others, like spam bots get your number or
address and plague you forever.

Once upon a time scary trolls
lived under bridges in our imaginations.
Now there are real internet trolls
that use offensive online language
and show up in blogs and web forums
causing you to fall flat on your Face book page.

In yesteryear, flavor referenced distinctive taste;
today elementary particles called quarks come in flavors too.
They are: top, down, strange, bottom, up, and charm.
The most recently discovered quark, the Higgs Boson,

known as the "God particle," helps give mass
to all the elementary particles that have mass

and generates the need for more new and repurposed words
for matter
and poets.

First Place

Diana Woodcock
Thunderstorm On The Zambezi

That afternoon on the Zambezi, I recalled the words of a mother's
warning, Seek shelter, leave the river. But there we were, being blown
to and fro – nowhere to go – the birds smarter than us, hidden away in
reedbeds, waterberry and sausage trees. Gentle breeze turned violent, we
all kept silent, huddled under rain ponchos like hippos with only eyes
exposed above the water's surface. But before we could drown or be
struck down, the storm turned around and left us, drenched but none the
worse for the ordeal. The sun returned to reveal birds and waterfowl, and
we got on with our task– to bask in electrifying surroundings pulsing with
germinating power. The space around us luminous, inviting us in as we
became, after the rain, each one of us that African jacana walking among
reedbeds like Jesus on water, inspecting each stalk for insects. We hung on
to the natural and beautiful, centered on each wondrous bird that passed
our way to stay in the moment, adrift on the Zambezi, after the storm,
its banks lined with thorn and fire, crocodiles and Nile monitor lizards,
baboons and waterbuck. What luck to be locked in the present – to look
from ground to sky and know when we die it'll all go on without us – each
thorny, flowering hedge at theriver's edge filled with light and the power
of possibility beyond catastrophe – as the Zambezi went on flowing, all
might and mystery, far from idly.

Second Place

M. Lee Alexander
Bem-Vinda A Florianópolis

Saturday is family day in Brazil, and everyone
  flees to the nearest park. Wanting to fit in I join them:
   riding my bicycle along the silt-sand crescent shore
    on the way to the botanical garden I stop for caldo de cana,
     sugarcane juice with lime squeezed fresh by the vendor
    who says "Bom dia, senhora, tudo bem?" "All is well?"

    At the garden I glimpse the orange flash of a rare toucan
    shrouded in the broad-leaved palms above my head, while
   beneath a family picnics in the central square of spiky grass.
  On their blanket a Brazilian feast: fresh sliced mango,
 passion fruit, cassava root tapiocas, pão de queijo (puffy
balls of breaded cheese) and brigadeiro chocolate tortes.

The middle child puts her face inside the empty oval
  of a painted outdoor sculpture shaped like open pages
  and says "Look Mamãe, I'm a book, come read me!"
   While Uncle in local colors of blue and white stripes
   for his home team known as "Lion of the Island"
    guides a soccer ball expertly round the clouded lake,

    And Auntie tells the baby those birds are called "Quero-quero,"
    because their cries call out incessantly "I want, I want!"
   So as daylight fades I push my tourist bike along the circled path
   and out the garden gate toward home and ready meals for one,
  with directions all in Portuguese which I am learning
phrase by singsong labyrinthine phrase.

First Place

Drury Wellford
Resistance

the cowlick above
my right temple   is eternal

no matter   how much
I pull it straight   with product

comb it down   with water
part my hair to the other side

the undulation always
reappears   like a stiff tsunami

the ghost of my curly
hair   now turned soft and grey

straight   not thick   dark   wild
all over the place

thinking it was   free
and could do whatever it wanted

like my young mind   my
character   decades ago

trying to flee the conformity
convention   and not-fitting-in of home

until now   beaten back by life
to where I started   safe but unstimulated

by sameness and   homogeneity
the ache of the cowlick   in my heart

Second Place

Anne Metcalf
Old China

For years, she put plates
whose sets numbered less than four,
mugs without matches,
and stainless steel, now superseded
by the newer non-stick,
into boxes marked "Country House!"
It was as much a dream as reality,
and she squirreled away for its inevitability
until one day, packing for a move,
her son looked up at her and asked,
"Did you and Dad once have a country house?"
Whereupon she had to admit,
No, they had not, that it had never come to be.
That there was no second kitchen
with empty shelves to fill.
No second chance to warm a cold aching space
with the promise of shared glances
and laughter around a long table
glinting with silver and crystal,
a complete china pattern,
painted with leaves and berries,
laid for twelve, maybe more!
A fire burning steadily
under an old mantel weighted with candles and pine.
Outside, deer foraging in the snow.

First Place

Ruth Holzer
Dutch And Dad

> Bronx-born compatriots,
> children of the new century,
> ignorant of one another.
> Who knows, they might even
> have celebrated their bar mitzvahs
> on the same day. We do know
> that both of them eluded the flu
> and grew up, Dutch to run
> a fleet of trucks hauling
> bootleg booze from Canada
> down to the thirsty cities,
> and Dad to study accounting
> in night school. Dutch had hitmen
> rub out his rivals; Dad worked
> behind his father's bar with only
> a baseball bat for protection.
> Dutch was lord of the numbers racket
> when Dad was trying to sell encyclopedias
> door to door in Newark, where Dutch
> was shot in a downtown chop house,
> while Dad stared at the infant in the crib,
> and wondered how he would feed it.

Second Place

Katharyn Howd Machan
Her Eyes Lit Amber Like A Fox

the hunter makes her way through old woods,
bow in hand, arrows ready, certain
today she will find the beast
with the horn that gored her father.
No one else believes he died
in quest of a silver fairy tale,
but she's his blood: they both knew
her grandmother's stories would come true
if they found the half-hidden path.
That one morning he went alone
he never returned, but a wild bird
came and sang hard at her window
and her heart saw four sharp hooves.
Basket of roses on her back,
watered wine, three crimson apples,
and on her feet thin sturdy shoes
heavy as iron, as prayer.
One night, two nights, three nights, four:
now she hears the distant whinny
like a taunt among branches and vines.
Already she feels the wisps of beard,
the mane like moonlight's path.
She will find her father's body.
And the beast who cannot exist but does
will disappear into her love
with words whispered soft and clear.

First Place

Sarah Kohrs
Hands, At Cuevas De Las Manos, Argentina

Hands, at Cuevas De Las Manos, Argentina
Prehistoric Cave Art

When all the world
was ice infringed upon
outcrops of pressed
corals and clams, caves
called man in like sirens
sucking masts toward
a place where flame danced.

Then—hands outstretched to touch
the hyang that flit in lines along the walls, steeped in
shadow-taunts, until one breath blew out ochre that fixed form:
the beginning of becoming

on a corpse road, whose
end harbors a stone stairway skyward. A place where there meets
here. And handprints animate like birds that wing about heaven's
mezuzah. Paintings posit

meaning from the moltenness
of it all—inspired by the first muse. It's a ritual of being,
quiescence in a womb of ice, star-gilded and steeped in
souls that wanted to linger.

Second Place

Adele Gardner
Night And Sleep

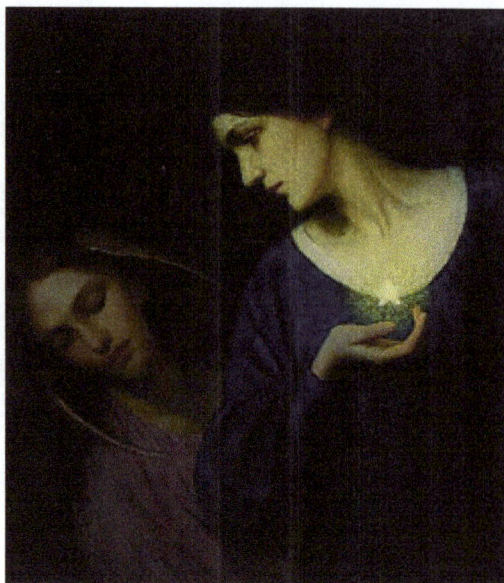

Night and Sleep
Mary Lizzie Macomber
August 21, 1861 - Feburary 4, 1916

Night, her gentle face lively
with the subtle fire of stars:
the ones in her eyes, the one at her breast,
gentled there, protected like the grown child
who slumbers now, always slumbers,
ever since she came of age, came into herself:
Sleep, my child.
Yes, Sleep—with Mother Nyx to guard
and guide your slumbers by starry light—
the gentle effect Night always has on the Slumberer,
their perfect alchemy making it possible
for even the insomniac to rest at times
from fevered labors,
brains fanned at last
by the wings at the temples of Sleep.
But Night never guessed it would be so hard
to only see her daughter in dreams.

First Place

Barbara Leary
These Birds

These birds will not fly: it's not a modern phenomenon.
They shed their down and feathers softly,
Their shunned bodies dull with longing.
If they start singing toward the sunlight
It will be because they live in darkness.

O you must not blaspheme what binds them!
They flock unquestioningly to fellowship and order.
They abide obediently in the airless buildings!
They wait and wait and wait for Him.
And never the feathers do fly nor the bodies do rise.

They sway as grasses, they murmur as flies,
Though they affect a contented and guileless mien—
It would be easy for them to leave, and that's what they crave.
Yet they bide, while their bones burn wild with desire
With eyes turned skyward, and will not fly for themselves.

After **Stillborn** by *Sylvia Plath*

Second Place

Ruth Holzer
Matinée Musicale

1. Impromptu

Through the maze of galleries,
you lead me back
to one painting I had missed:
a soft green and orange
wash of light reflected
on the shimmering surface
of a summer lake at dawn.

2. Romance

Too sweet, the violin's
solo avowal.
The orchestra
rejoices in variations
as it decorates
that single plaint.
Which one could live
without the other?

3. Fugue

The cool logic
of combination
and separation.
Intricate machinery
dissolves and
resolves again,
each time repeating
the same old problem
differently.

4. Albumblatt

A crumpled autumn leaf,
this page preserved past sense.

First Place

Sharon Ackerman
Children Picking Raspberries

Mostly I recall a carefulness of hand
 light bodies of honeybees
among the yet-to-be-fruit
blossoms. But slipping in,
finding the knobby red tip
loose and ready, knowing this is how
a berry should be picked.
More than that, slowness—
 a turning over in the mind,
working gently down a stem.
Amid the drone and sting of summer,
a warm jam of over-ripeness,
such a patina of childhood in the stained
palm! As if the sweet globes,
hundreds of them, could dangle so many days
in suspension, or their wild taste—
bright leaf and grit, coax the sun
to its setting, as our fingers let fly
into a pail, the truest thing
they would ever hold.

Second Place

April J. Asbury
Off The Path

Trees scar the sky, and the road bleeds
into shadow. You're lost,
and the wolves keen hunger
to an empty night.

There's no way home. No pebbles,
no breadcrumbs. The wolves
will catch you first. They feed
on fear and your softest parts;
they will clean your bones
with their long red tongues.

Before you die, you'll see those long-lost children,
half-covered by leaves, unnoticed by robins,
unmourned by sparrows. Is there comfort
in knowing you're not alone? Or will you see
only so much ivory: yellow, brown, white
as cream, smooth as moonlight
sifted through the trees?

First Place

Julia Travers
After

It all
peels back
into flakes
old metallic paint

grows translucent
insect wing in the dashboard

breaks down
soft autumn leaf
mauve, lavender confetti
underfoot.

Wholeness was just a word
spoken in the air.

When it comes to the work
of rearranging time for you,

I have no hands.

Second Place

Ruth Holzer
The Bent Fork

This is the fork
with the twisted tines
that I have inherited
along with other utensils.

Cleaning up after dinner once,
he seemed to have had enough
of her complaints about the meal
he'd made, or perhaps it was

something else, but the red mist
must have come down for a reason,
as it can descend upon
even the most gentle of natures,

and he grabbed the rack of dishes
he'd just washed, and dashed it to the floor
with a great clashing of knives
and smashing of glasses and plates.

As he shouted, he stomped
on everything, this fork too,
that I keep in a box
among my souvenirs.

Josee Winston-Feder
Sister Brook

I strain my ears to hear
a bubbling sound.
I start to follow the bubbling.
I find the little brook that runs
not too far from the ocean
near our house.
I dip my toes cautiously
into her cool, rushing water.
Her sandy floor
holds memories within.
I reach into my small bag
and pull out my goggles.
I place them on my head,
scrunch up my eyes,
and…Splash!
I jump in.
I slowly open my eyes
and feel her rippling water
surge behind me.
I let my body rise
to her surface.
I drink in a breath
and dive back down
towards her floor.
I thank her, silently,
for a beautiful day
of swimming.

Ariana Blake
Fool's Gold

Cold
The maritime souls passed around the treasure
Jewels too large and too stunning to measure
Though they will know jewels they'll never know love
Piles and piles of mother of pearl and coins of
Gold

Cold
The hardened spirits lurk at their old-time haunts
Loudly they argue as they exchange their taunts
They are slaves to gold, freedom not being mined
Digging and longing for the day they will find
Gold

Cold
The conquerors ride, each chased by his shadow
Each one on a quest to find El Dorado
Joy lost in the distance, worthless and tiny
The real desire for bright, bold, smooth, and shiny
Gold

Kestrel Linehan
Abecedarian For A Sunrise

A stream of gold sunlight
Barges into our tent.
Cranky faces trudge
Down towards the
Early sun.
Far across the ocean,
Geese flap their wings.
Hello, they say.
Islands surround us, their
Jagged rocks piercing the sea,
Keeping secrets for the tree
Limbs.
Morning wakes up,
Notices the girls watching her, and
Opens her yellow light. Lobster
Pots sway in the light breeze, and
Quarrelsome seagulls
Rise into the mist,
Stretching their wings over the ruby sky.
Tonight this
Umber sunrise will be gone,
Vanished, all its beauty turned into
Wishes for the next day:
Xanthous whisps
Yearning for more time,
Zig zagging through the dark night.

Sophia Fourquet
The Joy Of Paintings

I need to live in a Bob Ross painting.
With peaceful enormous mountains far away out yonder,
the pinnacle half secured by cheerful little mists,
a cheerful little tree and its numerous siblings and sisters
covering the scene of light snowfall and developing hedges.
A little lodge washed in liquifying snow rests easily
alongside a defrosting private lake lit by a cadmium yellow sun.
This is the place I need to live,
swarmed in shades of titanium white,
phthalo green and blue,
12 AM dark,
Alizarin ruby,
what's more, Indian yellow
where there are no mix-ups,
just upbeat mishaps,
where the important choices
don't matter.
What's more, the trials by fire are
where the following tree will go.
In a Bob Ross painting,
I could live calmly.

Laci Powell
Of The Things She Creates

I thank the earth for her magic and materials,
For soft damp soil and bone-dry sand.
For gorgeous stone creations, crystals and stalagmites.
Wildflower fields, rugged mountains, oceans cavernous.
Her skin nurtures and is nurtured—of greens, blues, and yellows.
And every life has roots that run deep.
Every event leads back to her, phenomena, disasters, miracles.
All that is here, from fossils to clouds.
Loud, silent; Large, microscopic; Aberrant, simple.
She creates and restricts, beauty both within and out.
A force of nature, and everything in between.

Claudia Martin
Little Red

A cardinal in the bushes,
Not snowy quite just yet.
May sound not as intriguing,
Yet it stands out from the rest.
You may associate them with winter,
Or with the coming of early spring.
But this cardinal chooses autumn
As the time to spread its wings.
Kind of funny to see,
You may laugh or scoff at the thought.
But this red is so much brighter
Than any leaf in fall.
They come for holly berries,
And to mate when spring is here.
But what do they come for,
When fall seems to appear?
They eat acorns like squirrels,
And they decide to live in peace.
Maybe they wanted to brag
About the pretty color they keep.
Yet I don't think that's it.
It must be something more.
Like casting a hook to fish,
Not knowing you caught the shore.
The mystery still awaits,
To be answered soon enough
These pretty little reds,
Like not to boast and bluff.
Perfect little birds,
They overview our state.
We see them quite a lot as they stay with their mates.
They keep by home for comfort,
Never out of grasp.
And soon they'll find the unfortunate soul,
And guide them along their path.

Collin Shiflett
Your Color Wheel

You're gone but still here,
floating among homes blanketed in powder snow.
The way you saw life with colors
still doesn't always make sense.
Your feelings were hues on a wheel
I struggled to decipher.
"How are you?"
"Light pink."
You didn't explain the emotion,
offering further information on the shade.
"Think the color of a pink orchid
as its first bud blooms."
Pink, a color of compassion and love
yet you were feuding with a friend that day.
The color of your flushed cheeks when she hung up.
Always breaking traditions, love was aquamarine.
Most of your colors rooted in nature.
Sadness, a light yellow. You saw the sun,
alone in the sky. We went to the park
on the cloudiest of days.
I look back at the day where you reached
for my hand and pulled me to a nearby bush.
I remember that big smile as you put your hand out
and the butterfly landed in your palm.
The photo I took was a green blur lifting
from the tip of your finger. Seeing that shade of green,
it was your happiness.
Many depict ghosts and spirits as white
or gray, but you're light blue. I feel it.

www.ingramcontent.com/pod-product-compliance
Lightning Source LLC
Chambersburg PA
CBHW072049040426
42447CB00012BB/3075